Foreword

I feel truly blessed to be involved in this divinely inspired process. This book serves to heighten our perceptions and send our lives in a new and important direction. Through essays, scriptures and parables filled with vital truths, the Nowlins celebrate the power of God and our connection to Him. We learn how to heal relationships and gain strength for living that comes from a deep and abiding faith. Our love for God emerges as a love for self and solidifies our worth as human beings, allowing us to love one another. Often we become weary from the weight of the world and forget how to interact with those who love us. At the end of each chapter of *Attitude Adjustment of the Christian Man and Woman* we are given practical steps that enable us to be more open and vulnerable with each other. Through this process we release pain and past disappointments ieading to fulfilling relationships, emotional and psychological stability and a sense of well being. This book is so appropriate at a time when the world is in turmoil and more families are broken. Arthur and Kim Nowlin have answered the call to do God's work, and He has much more in store for them. You will treasure this wise and encouraging book. Now, join me on the journey to spiritual enlightenment.

Debraha Watson, Ph.D.
2004

About the Book

It is our intention to offer you, the reader, an opportunity to develop techniques in order to make a paradigm shift for change. This book will assist in providing a spiritual experience required in addressing interpersonal baggage from family origin and challenges we face daily. We share our favorite scriptures that comfort us through our own personal difficulties. We incorporated short stories – taken from real life situations – to provide insight into addressing issues of trust, adversity and hope.

God is with us all, yet Kim and I have recognized how important it is to develop our own personal relationship with Him. This book will assist you by providing information from three perspectives: the Word, the authors, and you, the reader. We encourage you to allow the Holy Spirit to manifest in you from this reading experience. May God bless you as you encounter the *Attitude Adjustment of The Christian Man and Woman.*

THE ATTITUDE ADJUSTMENT
OF THE
CHRISTIAN MAN AND WOMAN

by Arthur and Kim Nowlin

xulon
PRESS

THE ATTITUDE ADJUSTMENT
OF THE CHRISTIAN MAN AND WOMAN

Published by Kim Logan Communications, Inc.
©2004 by Arthur and Kim Nowlin

Senior Editor – Jill McClure
Editor – Debraha Watson, Ph.D.
Cover Image by William Moore

Printed in the United States of America

ISBN 1-594679-64-9

Library of Congress Control Number: 2004099660
Library of Congress Control Number: TXU1028003

For information:
Kim Logan Communications, Inc.
8313 Grandriver Avenue
Detroit, Michigan 48204
(313) 898-8200
www.kimlogancommunications.com

www.xulonpress.com

Table of Contents

Dedication

This book is dedicated to you,
the family

Acknowledgements

Giving all honor to God for the opportunity to share this information, as a result of prayer, fasting, and seeking God's Holy Word.

Very special thanks to Debraha Watson, Jill McClure, Angela Baker and Deborah Rose for their many gifts and talents. To my sister, Reneé Humphreys, for her untiring diligence in the production of this book. To our children: Micha, Erin and Jason; and to family and friends, thank you for your prayers and support throughout this effort.

May the peace of God continue to be with you all.

Isaiah 55:11
So shall my word be that goeth forth out of my mouth;
it shall not return unto me void,
but it shall accomplish that which I please
and it shall prosper in the thing whereto I sent it.

Preface

A middle-aged couple, by the names of Curtis and Mary, had been married for many years. This couple had some differences, but in spite of it all, they loved each other. One day, Mary told Curtis she felt he had not forgiven her for a past mistake and he continued to hold the grudge in his heart. Curtis rarely spoke of the mistake to Mary, but she knew her husband still carried the pain. She prayed and they prayed together, but nothing seemed to help.

This barrier poured over into other issues such as trust and respect towards her husband. They continued to pray, worship, and serve God together, but because of their negative attitude towards the problem, they couldn't find a solution. As a result, they continued to allow self to interfere with their healing process.

Many times people give up on their relationship because of negative attitude towards the situation or problem. But what they continue to need is an ATTITUDE ADJUSTMENT in order to Break Barriers and Build Bridges towards their healing.

Curtis and Mary needed a solution to their problem, and they realized they couldn't do it alone. They needed help in order to heal. Their next step was to make the call for Christian counseling.

This book is being offered to assist couples, as well as individuals and families who may be experiencing personal difficulty within their households. Let us focus on addressing some of the issues and offer short-term options that will enhance the awareness from a personal perspective. We want to help you experience a spiritual change that will impact you individually and as an entire family.

Philippians 1:6
Being confident of this very thing, that he which hath begun a good work in you will perform it until the day of Jesus Christ.

Arthur & Kim Nowlin
Many names herein have been changed to protect
the privacy of our clients.

Chapter One
The Assault of Fear

Fear, Why is this a Barrier?

Fear is something that manifests itself within our character. It creates barriers to our achieving our personal goals and objectives. We need to recognize that fear exists. Also, we need to understand the tools needed to reconstruct our approach to fear in a healthy manner.

This brings us to the understanding and recognition of fear. We are unable to cope with circumstances that occur because of this barrier. Such understanding applies to our interpersonal relationships in the aspect of how we are seen and how we see others. The ability to move beyond fear is dependent on change from within ourselves. Fear impacts our lives in every aspect. If we are unable to address this barrier in a positive manner, it will be destructive within our life cycle. Through God, we have the power to turn fear into a learning tool once we understand its origin. God is strength, and our relationship with Him allows us to communicate our fears to Him and allows a release of its hold on us. Our Christian walk permits us to find comfort in Jesus.

Our inhibitions of fear must be turned over to the Lord before we can find the true meaning of God's love and how it provides protection in every aspect of our lives. The book of Matthew reminds us when Peter saw Jesus walking on the water, he became afraid. When Jesus called Peter to come, Peter, without thinking, had the faith he could walk to Jesus. But the moment Peter allowed fear – rather than faith – to take hold of his soul, his fear took him down into the water. When fear surrounds us, it can cause us to drown, like Peter sinking into the sea. (*Matthew 14:29,30*)

These are some barriers that can cause fear: being accepted by our peers, the fear of learning forgiveness of others, the fear of giving unconditional love. If we are unable to address these fears in a positive perspective, it can hinder our personal and moral development in maintaining a productive relationship with God, self, and others.

A Story is told...

Alexander just completed college and was provided an opportunity to acquire a very important job. One of his job priorities consisted of making presentations to the business community. Upon receiving his letter of acceptance to the position, he began to focus on his fears of public speaking. He started having anxiety attacks. He started telling himself, "I can't do it." He began putting negativity and defeat in his mind every day. As he continued to project this fear, his mother sensed his anxiety. She became very concerned.

Early one morning, she called Alexander into the room and said, "Son, I have a problem." Alexander responded, "What is it mother?" "My job is asking me to do presentations and I am so afraid, I don't think I can do this." Alexander looked at his mother in dismay. He dropped his head for a moment. Then a gleam came in his eyes and they embraced. Alexander then acknowledged, "Many days and nights I would drive by school. I felt like giving up, but I couldn't because you taught me I can do all things through Christ who strengthens me." (*Philippians 4:13*) "Mom, God promised us He would see us through the most difficult times in our lives. So Mom, you can do that presentation without fear." She looked at her son and said, "Alexander, so can you."

Have you ever experienced a fear, and it prevented you from achieving success?

II Timothy 1:7
*For God has not given us the spirit of fear; but of power,
and of love, and of a sound mind.*

What are my fears?

_____

_____

_____

The Challenge

Whose fight is it???

Face your inhibitions and trust in HIM
Experience the joy of allowing God to take control
Ask God to reveal to you His will
Rejoice and give God the glory for your victory

What Challenges am I facing today? Am I in a Tug of War and don't know why? What are some of the challenges I am facing in my life?

1. _____

2. _____

3. _____

4. _____

5. _____

Steps to Overcoming your Challenges
1. Prayer
2. Faith
3. Commitment to change
4. Taking action to resolve the challenge

II Chronicles 20:15
For the battle is not yours, it is the Lord's

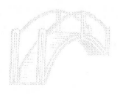

How Can I Endure The Challenges?

What I Need To Do:

I need to recognize the problem within my relationship.

_____

I need to recognize the origin of the problem.

_____

I need to recognize how the problem has manifested.

_____

I need to know what to do for resolution.

_____

_____

_____

_____

Issues of breakdown:
1. Lack of communication in the relationship.
2. Lack of spirituality in the relationship.
3. Lack of sensitivity shown within the relationship.
4. Lack of humility within the relationship.
5. Lack of understanding of my family dynamics (Family Origin).

Enhancing Awareness:
Do I recognize what needs to be done in my relationship?
Do I place the blame on someone else?
Do I allow issues to develop because we are not on
one accord?
Do I recognize what I need to maintain what I have?
Do I really know my mate?
Do I nurture my relationship with my mate?
Do I nurture my relationship with God?

• **Remember, a daily inventory of yourself and family can save many steps backwards.**

• **Remember, you are more than a Conqueror through Christ Jesus.**

• **Remember, you need to allow the Holy Spirit to control your emotions.**

Proverbs 25:28
He that have no rule over his own spirit
is like a city broken down and without walls.

Proverbs 25:24
It is better to dwell in the corner of a house top
than with a brawling woman in a wider house.

The difficulties in implementing behavioral changes during crisis situations can create stress, which may require professional Christian intervention. Recognizing the situation that exists can cause health issues and present danger to your lifestyle.

The chart below has a breakdown of the different types of abuse that an individual may experience in his or her life.

Types of Abuse		
Mental	Physical	Sexual
Self Inflicted abuse	Substance abuse	Verbal

Working through Rejection		
Enhancing Self Esteem	Eliminating Isolation	Eliminating Depression
Eliminating Lack of Confidence	Eliminating Anxiety	Eliminating Fear

Everybody is going through but I'm going to break through		
Build-up the Spiritual Character	Build-up the Emotional Character	Build-up the Physical Character

@Arthur & Kim Nowlin

No weapon that is formed against thee shall prosper...
Isaiah 54:17

Many of our clients come to us out of different circumstances and for different needs. Quite often, however, as we continue to address their issues, the existence of some form of abuse becomes prevalent. Our questions to you are:

1. Have you ever been abused?
2. Are you able to talk about it?
3. Are you ready to work through the abuse?
4. How do you find help?

Personal Notes

_____

_____

_____

_____

_____

_____

_____

_____

_____

_____

_____

_____

_____

_____

_____

_____

_____

_____

_____

Chapter Two
Struggling through...

Struggling through Trust,
Deceit, betrayal, shame, and guilt

Trust is an intimate relationship between self and others that can develop into a protective sensitive place of belonging. It is appropriate to believe that a lack of trust creates a false sense of security which illuminates into other behavioral deficiencies, such as deceit, betrayal, shame, guilt, and the loss of caring.

In the development of trust, we have to reflect back to our family origin. As a child in most families, we were nurtured and cared for without any reservation, and provided with unconditional love. Until this feeling of security was violated, we were comfortable with our trust and love for others at that specific time in our lives. The significance is: when the trust was broken. Unfortunately for many of us, this created a barrier for establishing positive relationships. The difficulty then, of unconditional love, is impacted by an accumulation of barriers which prevents us from progressing and acquiring a meaningful sense of self.

Our relationship with God offers us an alternative to regaining trust of self and others. Moses was in the desert and heard the cries of the children of Israel because they were thirsty (*Numbers 20:9-11*). He prayed to the Lord and was provided an answer. God told Moses to take his rod and "gather thou the assembly together, thou, and Aaron thy brother, and speak ye unto the rock before their eyes; and it shall give forth his water and thou shalt bring forth to them water out of the rock: so thou shalt give the congregation and their beasts drink. (*Numbers 20:11*), Moses lifted up his hand, and with his rod he smote the rock twice: and the water came out abundantly, and the congregation drank and their beasts also."

Moses' sense of anger heightened because of the children of Israel's doubt. Moses lost his self-control and reacted out of rage, going against God's will. Moses forgot his relationship with God, only for a moment, and that moment of anger caused great consequences, which prevented him from entering into the promised land. (*Numbers 20:12*) The relationships we have with others should reflect what God represents in our lives. Anger will cause great distress and place us in a vulnerable position, causing us to lose faith and trust in God. Without God, there is only destruction.

God does not want us to have destruction in our lives. He wants us to trust in Him. He will give guidance in every aspect of our existence. He has the power to provide us with all of our wants and needs. If we, as Christians, want to receive the power from the Lord, we must learn to trust in Him, and **"We must learn to Let Go and Let God."**

To improve our ability to trust others will require us to feel good about ourselves. The realization of trusting ourselves will rejuvenate our self-esteem and increase our ability to make good judgments of situations, and of people.

We, as humans born into this world as sinners, must recognize the relationship between self-esteem and trust as components of our whole self. Each aspect of these components is manifested from the spiritual self. Some of us are able to understand this ailment of our spiritual relationship with God and our human construct earlier than others. Once this relationship has been nurtured through prayer, we are able to benefit from the whole armor of God. This will also enhance our ability to trust God and lean on Him. We will not have inhibitions regarding who we can trust. We will be able to understand that our trust is first in our relationship with God.

Once this is established, a certain sense of serenity becomes clear through our relationship with God. It is not important that we focus on someone violating the trust established in the relationship, because it is clear that through their humanistic tendencies, they become fallible, as we are all fallible. Recognizing this, we must be open to the Holy Spirit so that He can work in us to forgive others and ourselves.

Proverbs 3:5,6
Trust in the Lord with all thine heart; and lean not unto thine own understanding. In all thy ways acknowledge him, and he shall direct thy paths.

Shame & Guilt:
Releasing the Guilt and Shame in your life

We relate to people with either an "open door" or "closed door" policy.

A closed door conceals the negativity of our past:
- Shame
- Betrayal
- Burdens
- Unforgiveness
- Guilt
- Depression

An open door signifies our recognizing:
God has forgiven us, therefore, we must forgive ourselves
- Forgiveness
- It is in the past
- Rebirth
- Let it go
- I'm free

Do I have someone who's keeping me bound to a negative past?

_____

_____

_____

_____

_____

It's time to move on!
It is over. Remember, You are Forgiven.
Don't allow anyone or anything to keep you bound
and living in the past.

Time is moving on! And you need to move with it...

A Story is told...

A few years ago, a woman named Judith walked into our office. She appeared very worried. The conversation began with Judith discussing a concern about her only daughter, Elaine.

Judith always allowed Elaine to demonstrate independence, but she was concerned about her daughter's association with a young man of less than appropriate upbringing. One day, Elaine told her mother she and one of her girlfriends were going to the park. Her mother told her to be home by a certain time. The time came for the daughter's return home, but she hadn't arrived. Judith became concerned and called over to the girlfriend's home. The mother answered and informed Judith her own daughter was out of town for the weekend. Shortly after the telephone conversation, Elaine walked in the door. When asked where she had been, the daughter replied, "With my girlfriend at the park." Judith slowly sat down on the sofa and began to cry. Elaine asked her mother if she was all right.

When the response was "No", Elaine questioned, "What's wrong, where does it hurt? Are you in pain mother?" Judith answered, "Yes, you have violated my trust. While I was waiting for you, I called over to your friend's home and her mother told me her daughter was out of town for the weekend. Then I knew who you were with." With tears in her eyes, her mother asked, "How do we rebuild the trust?"

Judith felt she needed help to rebuild the trust in her relationship with Elaine. Her concern was allowing her daughter to experience independence after she violated the trust.

A mother will always love her child no matter what;
for a mother's love is endless,
as God's love is for you and I.

Psalms 119:133
Order my steps in thy word:
and let not any iniquity have dominion over me.

Rebuilding the Trust

The mother was hurt by the lies her daughter had told her. After years of having a trusting relationship, suddenly things changed. Even with the Holy Spirit revealing the situation to the mother, it became clear that a decision was needed to reestablish their relationship. **Now, God must step in.**

The process of taking a risk to regain trust becomes difficult because of our human frailty. Imagine how Christ felt when he told Peter that he would deny him three times. Christ was hurt, yet understood Peter's lack of trust in his faith. Christ recognized that Peter had to experience the "tests" before him. He knew such development was essential to Peter becoming a strong foundation in the building of His church. Christ died on the cross asking His Father to forgive those who sin against Him. Christ became the sacrifice, the Lamb of God.

We must learn to forgive and take the risk of establishing trust by nurturing and building a new trust through the spiritual relationship of our Christian walk.

Proverbs 3:5,6 provides a clear process for establishing a new trust and a better relationship by trusting in the Lord. Remember that the risk in this endeavor will require you to build a bridge from the foundation, and it will take patience and work to be successful.

Christ represents the bridge in our lives. We have the choice to eliminate the barriers in our lives through Jesus Christ. To build the foundation you must work towards building new bridges and breaking down barriers in your life.

• **What choices are you making for your life, and will the choices you make reflect the life of Christ?**

These are the life choices that I should make in order to build new bridges and break down the barriers in my life:

1. _____

_____

2. _____

_____

3. _____

_____

4. _____

_____

Letting go of "Old Baggage"

There are times in our lives when we may feel our "baggage" is valuable – the things we feel to be essential. Some of the things we consider significant or necessary may need to be reassessed.

For example: Is verbal abuse something you need to re-evaluate and eliminate from your relationships? You may need to self-evaluate the issues in your life that can become negative "baggage".

**In some relationships, men and women carry baggage.
Which one are you?**

Am I...?
Living with mistrust? *Yes_____ No_____*
Living with lies? *Yes_____ No_____*
Living with abuse? *Yes_____ No_____*
Living with deception? *Yes_____ No_____*
Living with pain? *Yes_____ No_____*
Living with misery? *Yes_____ No_____*
Living with hurt? *Yes_____ No_____*
Living with secrets? *Yes_____ No_____*

**Carrying baggage from one relationship to another?
With Christ, barriers are broken and
your healing process begins**

I need to confront my issues.
I need to allow God to put them in the past.
I need to move on towards building a better life.

Jeremiah 29:11
*For I know the thoughts that I think towards you,
and the Lord's thoughts of peace and not evil
to give you an expected end.*

Personal Notes

Tools Towards Rebuilding Trust...

1. Pray and Fast. What are you praying about? Be specific in your prayer requests.

What are my issues? _____

_____

_____

2. Allow God to help you develop an action plan to follow.

*What are my goals?*_____

_____

_____

3. Take the action step.

When am I willing to implement change? _____

_____

_____

4. Change your behavior.

How do I respond to what has impacted
my environment, others and myself? _____

_____

_____

_____

5. Am I being taken for granted? If so, in what ways?

_____

_____

_____

6. Do I have compassion, love, sensitivity, support, fun, time, structure and peace in my life? If not, how do I plan to obtain these things for myself?

_____

_____

_____

7. Change the communication process.

Am I willing to listen?
Am I willing to use time management for communicating?
What type of tone do I use when I communicate?

_____

_____

_____

_____

_____

Tools Towards Rebuilding Trust... (Continued)

8. Take time to learn yourself.

What are my needs? _____

_____

_____

*Are my needs being met?_____ Can I communicate my needs?_____
Are my needs realistic?_____*

9. Take time to learn about others and yourself.

Do I understand the personality of those living in my household?

_____

_____

10. Try to eliminate unnecessary stress.

What are my alternatives? _____

_____

_____

11. Consider professional intervention.
       Is therapy an option for you? _____
              Pastoral Counseling _____
              Therapeutic Christian Counseling _____
              Psychological Therapy _____
              Psychiatric Therapy _____

12. *Do I need someone to talk to? Yes_____ No_____*

Personal Notes

Personal Notes

Chapter Three
The "I Syndrome"

I and I Alone

It is apparent when we look at ourselves from the perspective of self-adulation, we become isolated from the reality of a normal caring lifestyle towards others. It is important to recognize the negative tendencies associated with arrogance and selfishness creating what we refer to as the "I Syndrome."

The question becomes: How do we address the issue of self in a manner in which it becomes healthy enough to motivate a behavioral change?

This will require a risk taking action to eliminate negative character defects and replace them with positive self development, such as becoming loving towards others, and putting self in its proper perspective.

The next concern regarding the "I Syndrome" is the establishment of the ego as a power generated from within ourselves. A defense mechanism is constructed because of the shame of being vulnerable to others. This ego is also a reflection of the absence of a relationship with the Holy Spirit.

Jesus Christ demonstrated a humble and loving spirit during his time on earth. During the time the devil tempted Jesus in the desert, he offered Jesus all the earthly treasures a man could desire. (*Matthew 4:1-11*) The temptation was futile for the devil, because there was nothing of value to destroy the relationship Jesus had with His Father. We should not allow any temptation to separate us from our joint inheritance to be shared with Jesus Christ. (*Romans 8:16,17*)

The key towards understanding ourselves is in our relationship with God. This will manifest itself as protection against temptation and self-gratification, establishing a spiritual connection between the Holy Spirit and our individuality. The lack of remorse of our personal transgressions towards God prevents us from interpreting and receiving His design for our lives. This will create further turmoil in our lives which will move us to rely on ourselves in our efforts to control our own destiny. We then alienate ourselves and succumb to the "I Syndrome".

Ask yourself the question, "Am I in the way of my blessing?"
Yes_____ No_____

**If your answer is yes, then do the right thing and
"Get out of your own way."**

The "I Syndrome" can take on many forms such as embellishing personal accomplishments, taking advantage of leadership positions, and determining there is no need for you to rely on faith or religious beliefs. The "I Syndrome" person is convinced he is superior to anyone else, including God.

If you can recognize that your attitude is not pleasing to God, then you are ready for an Attitude Adjustment. The "I Syndrome" will now become the will of God.

Adjusting the "I Syndrome" to "God's Syndrome"
1. Listen to others
2. Share with others
3. Learn how to demonstrate humility
4. Be sensitive to the needs of others
5. Be willing to give of yourself

Romans 12:1,2
I Beseech you, therefore, brethren, by the mercies of God, that ye present your bodies a living sacrifice, holy, acceptable unto God which is your reasonable service. And be ye not conformed to this world: but be ye transformed by the renewing of your mind, that ye may prove what is good, and acceptable perfect will of God.

**Do those within your environment hear
what you are trying to say?
Are you sensitive towards their needs?**

Yes_____ No_____

A Story is told...

A hardworking couple ran a dry-cleaning business in a poor community. They lived in the same building. Every day they would have juice and hot rolls for their customers. They operated this business for over twelve years and everyone knew their names and cared for the couple.

One day, another company offered to buy their business. This caused great distress to the couple because they didn't want to leave, as they had grown very fond of their friends and customers. However, they did sell the business, after receiving a lucrative offer.

The new owner was cold and non-caring towards his customers, and would consistently speak to them of his great accomplishments. He was unwilling to listen and share with his customers; he kept reminding them that this was his fourth business and he would be purchasing another dry-cleaners in a few weeks...

Over the course of time, customers stopped patronizing the new owner and business began to deteriorate. One day, the new owner became aware of another dry-cleaners in the community. He was told of previous customers taking business there, so he decided to see for himself what was attracting his customers to the "new" cleaners. When he walked in he was startled. There was juice and fresh hot rolls on the table, and there – behind the counter – was the hard working couple smiling and greeting their old friends and customers.

Clearly, the couple had learned over the years that relationships formed in the community were more important to their business than the financial gain.

Proverbs 18:12
Pride ends in destruction, humility ends in honor.

• **Are you facing destruction because of the "I Syndrome"?**

Personal Notes

Personal Notes

Chapter Four
Interpersonal Restoration

Restoration of Self

In restoring self, we must be able to determine the level of damage that has been impacted by our lifestyles. This restoration process requires diligent work towards behavioral reconstruction.

The restoration steps are prayer, study of God's Word, faith, plan development, and a vision of success. These steps are interwoven to create a rebirth and reconciliation towards God, self, and others. Continuing to pursue reconciliation requires increased listening capabilities to prepare our instincts for a self-assuring outcome.

In developing a plan, we must understand the goals and objectives required to be successful in the restoration process, and be completely committed and attentive to its implementation.

What becomes a barrier in this process of restoration is our lack of faith and willingness to obey God. Understanding that God can reconstruct our entire character should encourage us to divert from thoughts, words and actions associated with failure.

God wants you to be successful because He has designed a plan for each one of our lives. This plan must be fulfilled and completed to its full potential. It is important for us to recognize that when we fall short of our destiny, we are not bound to remain in that state of being. Get up and go forth. There are no limitations preventing your success "but you."

Steps towards Restoration
Prayer... Open communication with God
Action... Following the will of God
Plan... Developing goals and objectives designed by God
Success... Total submission to God

Philippians 1:6
Being confident of this very thing, that he which hath begun a good work in you will perform it until the day of Jesus Christ.

A Story is told...

A few months ago we had the pleasure of visiting an elderly man by the name of Paul Anthony. Mr. Anthony had been retired from his job for five years and lived on a fixed income. All his life he had cared for his family, and, six months prior to our visit, his wife had passed away. He was a faithful man and strong in his convictions to the Lord. He always had a smile on his face and always had something good to say about everyone he met.

Mr. Anthony told us that one sunny afternoon there was a knock on the door. The visitor introduced himself as being from the IRS, and indicated the house would be sold in ninety days for back taxes. Knowing he had always paid his bills and taxes on time, Mr. Anthony became confused when the IRS representative asked for the past receipts. He did not know where the receipts were and was unable to find them. With that, he was given ninety days to pay or vacate the property.

After the man left, Mr. Anthony began to pray. He opened his line of communication to God and had faith. He knew without a doubt he had paid the taxes.

Hebrews 11:1
Faith is the substance of things hoped for
and the evidence of things not seen.

Almost three months went by and with only two days left, his neighbors grew concerned, yet, despite the seriousness, Mr. Anthony kept his faith and cheerful countenance. With only one day left, the IRS man returned. Mr. Anthony stated, "I have one more day." The representative stated, "I know. I just came by to put up the 'For Sale' sign." "Well then," was the response, "would you like to come in and have some tea?" Graciously the man accepted. Mr. Anthony engaged in pleasant conversation, "Before my wife passed, she would make a very special herbal tea for me. I will make us some."

As he began to prepare the tea, he noticed old tea boxes on the shelf, and remembered his wife had kept important papers there... He began searching through the boxes and found the tax papers and receipts his wife had safely put away. Calmly, he went back to his guest, offered the tea and said, "I felt that you would find this to be interesting reading material, stamped with: Taxes paid in full."

The faith of Mr. Anthony was enough to keep him encouraged through a difficult time. We all have trials and tribulations throughout our lives. But, what becomes important during those experiences is how strong our relationship is with God.

Hebrews 11:6
And God is a rewarder of them that diligently seek Him.

Necessary Tools to Complete your Bridge

ACTION STEPS

1. Believe in yourself.
2. Prepare all necessary tools to accomplish goals and objectives.
3. Choose positive associations and make positive contacts.
4. Trust God in all your decisions.
5. Be prepared to move to the next level of your success.

Rewards are given to those who demonstrate the special fruits.

What are these fruits?
Galatians 5:22,23

1. _____

2. _____

3. _____

4. _____

5. _____

6. _____

7. _____

8. _____

9. _____

What's on your bridge?
Where is your bridge taking you?

Necessary Tools to Maintain your Bridge

When you are building a bridge, it is important to have all your tools, or your bridge will collapse.

Foundation... *Jesus Christ*
Blueprints... *Prayer*
Concrete... *Faith*
Sledgehammer... *Word of God*
Bolts... *Love*
Mortar... *Your relationship with God*
Water... *Holy Spirit*

What can you add in building your foundation with Christ?

1. _____

2. _____

3. _____

What Obstacles are in your way?

1. _____

2. _____

3. _____

What Motivators do you use in your daily life?

1. _____

2. _____

3. _____

Now it's your turn to build your own bridge
You can find the materials required for building
your personal bridge through faith.

Here's an example of what could be on your bridge

1. Forgiveness is
   the Plan

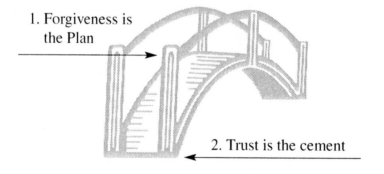

2. Trust is the cement

What are the next supplies needed
for you to construct your bridge?

_____

_____

_____

Personal Notes

Chapter Five
Essence of Patience

"The Wait Station"
How to get your breakthrough... when there is no way through

The "Wait Station" is a place where we rejuvenate all the information that contributed to the transformation process of you becoming whole. Now we are preparing ourselves to move to another level of development which will produce behavior that is new and different.

Two obstacles preventing us from implementing change are: our lack of faith and apathy. It is important we become motivated and rejoice in the new creature that the Lord will create. This implies that we can be changed and no matter what we are going through, the Lord is there to pull us through.

Micah 7:7
Therefore wait I say, wait on the Lord.

How often have you told yourself, "I need a breakthrough to overcome this difficult situation!! I am at my weakest moment, on my last nerve and at wit's end!!" You begin to burden yourself with worry because you want to escape the situation causing you distress, and as time evolves without resolution, the worry only intensifies...

There is a major barrier you must overcome before you obtain the breakthrough. You must prevent the barrier of worry. How do we do this? We trust in the Lord in how He will bring us through.

A young lady came to our office with concerns she had regarding her husband. It seemed to her he demonstrated little motivation when it came to resolving issues in the household. She claimed she became distressed when bills were not paid, and creditors continued to call about payments. Her husband's passive response was irritating to her, because he indicated they "needed to trust in the Lord and He would provide." While the husband worked overtime to get out of debt, it was taking too much out of the marriage. The stress was causing barriers in her relationship. She was unable to see the blessing God was providing her and did not want to wait on the Lord.

Her husband was not compelled to the barrier of worry. He believed the Lord would provide an answer, and the Lord did. The overtime was available. There was no sickness in the family, and God was in control. The young lady had to be open to change her way of believing and open herself up to the profound presence of the Lord. She had to learn how to recognize her breakthrough.

In the book of *John, Chapter 5, verses 1-17*, a man had an affliction for over thirty-eight years of his life. He had lain by a pool of water for a very long time, unable get in. It was believed that, at this particular pool, an angel came by from time to time to stir the water, and when that moment came, whoever first entered the pool was instantly cured of their infirmities. One Sabbath, Jesus saw the man lying next to the pool and asked him if he wanted to be made whole. The man's first response was that he was unable to get in the pool because he could not move fast enough and someone would always push him away. Yet, this man continued to wait on his healing and never stopped believing he could be healed. On this particular day, Jesus told the man to "Rise take up thy bed and walk" (*John 5:11*). The man got up and walked! Jesus healed him on the Sabbath, and while many persons witnessed the miracle, they wanted to kill Jesus because of this deed.

The man never stopped believing he would be healed, and he found his breakthrough in Jesus. The others, unfortunately, were unable to recognize the blessing: the barrier of hate bound them.

We must continue to trust in God when we are looking for our breakthrough. It becomes important for us to pray, fast, and meditate to be able to communicate with God.

Another important key is to learn how to be still while in the "Wait Station." God is God all by Himself. Once we are able to increase our understanding of God's will, we will be able to develop in our spiritual growth and receive our breakthrough when there is no way through.

Defining our EGO'S

1. The positive ingredients: E.G.O. (*Enhancing God Only*)
2. The negative ingredients: E.G.O. (*Edging God Out*)

The following steps will assist in developing our spiritual relationship with God and recognizing our breakthrough.

1. Develop skills of patience.

While you wait, you become renewed in body and spirit. A manifestation of the positive attributes of the Christian man and woman comes alive. Satan wants you to act on impulse.

Wait Station... Are you ready or are you having doubts?
Maybe???
I don't know... I'm always having doubts!!!
It happens to other people but not me.
When is my blessing coming?

Going through the *"Wait"* process:

2. Pray for wisdom.

Be specific as to what you ask for. When we can't see a way through the pain, we become stagnated, frustrated and confused. We must let God direct our path.

What do I need patience in? _____

_____

_____

Proverbs 3:5,6
...Trust in the Lord with all thine heart; and lean not on thine own understanding. In all thy ways acknowledge him, and he shall direct thy paths.

3. Ask God to grant you the ability to demonstrate humility.

Be open to receive the response needed to move on to the next level. Learn to yield, compromise, and withdraw (pull back) so that problems can begin to be resolved.

*What problems need resolution in my life?*_____

_____

_____

_____

_____

_____

_____

_____

Steps towards the Personal Breakthrough

How do you get a breakthrough
when you need relief from a problem?

Let's define breakthrough: *A release from a problem or burden. Learning how to see things from a different perspective.*

Promise Station... Believing and Receiving the Promises
My blessing is on the way!
Territory increased!
Showers of blessings!!!

1. Learn how to be still. Anxiety is high when problems occur.

What are the consequences of moving without God?

_____

_____

_____

2. Redirect your focus.
Prepare yourself by thinking positive. Read *Philippians 3:14*

My problems can be resolved when I.... _____

_____

_____

_____

_____

Family Breakthroughs

It becomes important to understand that families go through crises and experience serious difficulties. The need to overcome these situations remains with our ability to focus on the origin of the crisis and establish options for change. The family structure becomes significant in implementing redirected energy for a positive paradigm shift.

Reestablishing a new boundary of change in the dysfunctional family will require a risk taking procedure. Understanding the origin of the crisis is essential before any change can occur. Acknowledging the situation causing concern must be addressed openly within the family. Finally, a plan of action will be required to support the family decisions.

Psalm 9:9
The Lord is a refuge for the oppressed,
a stronghold in a time of trouble.

Important tools during the family crisis are: prayer on a daily basis, meditation, and fasting. Each component increases the spiritual power of the family looking for a breakthrough. A breakthrough requires constant communication with the Lord, and continued faith in his healing power. Prayer, meditation, and fasting are the first initial steps towards improving family dynamics and for redeveloping the family bond.

Let's talk about the concern and understand what the options are for change. It is important to discuss what happened within the structure, what damage occurred and what it will take to move forward. Once initial communication is developed, the pain can be released, and trust can slowly manifest out of the process. If trust is broken, the family will have difficulty understanding how to move to another level of forgiveness. How does a family forgive the devastation of substance abuse, physical abuse, verbal abuse or child abuse? The damage done appears irreversible. Therefore, it is crucial the family pray, meditate and fast during the first steps towards the healing. The family alone may have difficulty forgiving, but through the Spirit of the Lord, they can begin to move forward.

Luke 17:3,4
Jesus said, "If your brother sins, rebuke him, and if he repents forgive him. If he sins against you seven times in a day, and seven times comes back to you and says, I repent, forgive him."

After the spirit of forgiveness has been established, the family must move to a state of understanding, and recognize the realization of the human tendency to fall short of its objectives. The family must not be discouraged. It is important to continue to focus on achieving the goal of healing. The breakthrough has been established through the family's ability to come together to address the issues affecting the family dynamics. Restoration is in process, and determination becomes the motivation for finding the breakthrough.

Steps towards the Family Breakthrough

1. Pray, meditate, and fast about the family crisis
   (Seek you first the Kingdom of God. Matthew 6:33)
2. Understand the origin of the family crisis
3. Openly communicate about the particular issues causing concern

• **Tips to Remember**
3. Forgive others for their past mistakes
4. Restoration – is essential to restoring the love in the family
5. Motivation – maintains the desire for positive change
6. Determination – be steadfast and focused on success to achieve your breakthrough

II Timothy 3:12
Everyone who wants to live a life in Christ Jesus is persecuted
It's time for my breakthrough!!!

A Story is told...

Pastor James Charles was newly appointed to a congregation, and in order to get to church, he could only travel by bus. The bus station was located on the outskirts of the city. There, people from all walks of life waited to leave for their various destinations.

One day, he noticed a young couple surrounded by several suitcases. They seemed nervous and uncomfortable. For about twenty minutes, he watched while they waited for their bus to come. Finally, he approached them. He greeted them, and they nodded in acknowledgement. He told them he was on his way to his new church and admitted feeling nervous about the new experience. Opening up to him, the couple mentioned they were on their way to the city to find work. They didn't have much money and didn't have a place to live. Pastor Charles asked them which church they belonged to, and they answered, "We don't." He invited them to his church for dinner. They hesitated but said, "Yes, and thank you", and followed him onto the bus.

They talked about faith and their relationship with God. The couple felt relief and joy to know that someone cared about them. That evening, they were offered dinner, a place to live, and employment by members of the church.

The day began as a "no-promise" day for this couple. They had been at the bus station among strangers when the Lord interceded and opened a door to the "next" station – finding God, a new church family, a home, and employment. The Lord became the outside intercessor who assisted with their personal change – the "change Agent." Pastor Charles served only to enhance God's intercession.

God wants us to be His servants and to lead others to His Kingdom. As God's people, our love and caring for others should be demonstrated in our character at all times to bring glory to God.

Galatians 6:10
As we have opportunity, let us do good to all people
especially to those who belong to
the family of believers.

Personal Notes

Chapter Six
Modifying your Attitude

Breaking to Building

We have been preparing you, the reader, for the reconstruction of self. We have developed three key points to help in the transformation.

1. Preparing ourselves through prayer.
2. Being still to receive a blessing.
3. Practicing our transformation.

Each point reflects the positive ingredients in developing prayer, faith, self-esteem and spiritual awakening. Reflecting on the previous chapters, we must be able to recognize our behavior flaws and the need for an Attitude Adjustment in order to have spiritual development and success. We must also recognize the steps required in this change process.

After recognition of these points, steps towards self reconciliation consist of:

1. Openness to change.
2. Active participation towards change.
3. The ability to forgive self and others.
4. Demonstrating humility and compassion towards others.

Consistent communication with God provides us the energy to address the complex issues – those issues which previously caused defects in character and resulted in poor decision-making in the past.

The rejuvenation of mind, body, and spirit ensures us that our relationship with God is a continual reminder of the joy and peace needed as we cross the bridge of life.

In order to improve my attitude,
I must improve my relationship with God by.... _____

_____

_____

_____

To modify my attitude, I must feel the presence of God at my weakest moments as I am close to sin. I must develop a "Safety Plan" to call my Savior. What is my safety plan?

_____

_____

_____

_____

This is my favorite scripture*: _____

_____

_____

_____

_____

_____

*Recite your favorite scripture five times a day.

Am I open to change?
Am I demonstrating humility and compassion?

What to do when we are not talking!

When communication has broken down in a relationship, it becomes critical to take a new approach to those sensitive issues causing distress. It becomes essential to implement a change in how the communication is processed, and to use cautious judgement when evaluating the content of our dialogue. There is also a need for a risk taking experience towards rebuilding the communication between the two parties. Who will be the one to start the healing journey? Sometimes, the journey can be difficult with many obstacles. At other times there may only be a few issues to resolve. The significance of timing depends on the elapsed period before the initiation of the resolution. This is critical because it is a high priority that our issues are clear for recall and can be addressed.

Time is critical when unresolved issues exist in relationships. If discussion is not implemented towards reestablishing the communication in an appropriate time frame, frustration continues to manifest itself through anger, resulting in low self-esteem issues, and leading towards misinterpretation of actions. The slightest annoyance can be perceived as a direct attack on the partner's mind, body, and spirit. The need to correct this behavior will only come about when one partner comes out of his or her comfort zone and addresses the communication breakdown.

How do we begin healing without a positive communication process? We begin by doing what we need to do: communicate! The initial step towards effective communication is developing the ability to reason out the process within our inner-self, and learning what can be done to improve the exchange process. We have it broken down into four main points.

1. Developing effective communication may call for a self-inventory to determine how the communication is delivered – such as body language, voice tone, and self-control. Don't act on impulse during conflict. If your feelings are negative, take time to regroup.

In my self-inventory, I am learning the following about myself:

_____

_____

_____

**Listen to the Lord.
Develop your prayer life.
Involve yourself in a prayer group for support.**

2. Look at taking a risk and opening the communication with the belief that your efforts will establish change.

**Your belief for positive communication
demonstrates
your faith in God.**

I can do all things in Christ!

3. Don't be discouraged if the engagement does not go in the direction you expect. What becomes important is the positive actions demonstrated. Continue to focus on resolving the differences. Sometimes change is a slow process.

*If I become discouraged, I will remember
God is my strength when I trust in Him.*

4. If the process of communication remains stagnated, don't hesitate to obtain a qualified mediator to assist in eliminating the barrier.

Remember that in the process of relationships, positive communication can *"Make it last Forever"*

1. *What was my first step towards change?*

_____

_____

_____

2. *Did I pray for God's counsel?*
These are the significant points of my prayer:

_____

_____

_____

3. *Have I done all I can do to reestablish communication?*

_____

_____

_____

4. *Are my feelings controlling my attitude?*
If yes, what must I do for change?

_____

_____

_____

"Techniques for Rebuilding the Christian Family"

I. Spiritual Fitness

    A. <u>Communicate</u> with God through prayer – *(Matthew 7:7)*

    B. <u>Demonstrate</u> Christian Character – *(Galatians 5:22,23)*
       1. Respect & Thoughtfulness – *(1 Peter 3:8)*
       2. Kindness – *(Matthew 5:9)*
          Blessed are the Peacemakers, for they shall be called the children of God.
       3. Love – *(1 Corinthians 13:4)*
          Love is patient and kind, never envious or jealous.

    C. Let <u>go</u> of Negative Relationships –
       (Psalm 34:19; Philippians 3:13,14)

II. Attitude Adjustment

    A. <u>Recognize</u> the Problem – *(Ephesians 4:25)*

    B. Take <u>Action</u> – *(II Timothy 1:7)*

    C. Visualize <u>Change</u> – *(Hebrews 11:1,6; Ephesians 3:20)*

III. Expecting The "Promise"

    A. Take a <u>daily</u> inventory – *(II Timothy 2:15)*

    B. <u>Balance</u> and Deliverance – *(Romans 8:28)*

    C. Live a <u>Victorious Life</u> – *(Philippians 1:6)*

What techniques are you using?
Do you see a positive change in your family?

1. Technique: _____

_____

Do I see positive changes? _____

_____

2. Technique: _____

_____

Do I see positive changes? _____

_____

3. Technique: _____

_____

Do I see positive changes? _____

_____

4. Technique: _____

_____

Do I see positive changes? _____

_____

Personal Notes

_____

_____

_____

_____

_____

_____

_____

_____

_____

_____

_____

_____

_____

_____

_____

_____

Personal Notes

Chapter Seven
Developing Spiritual Sensory

Connecting God... Me... Myself... and I

This chapter will act as a catalyst to assist you in the process of implementing behavioral change through God, and self-actualization within the positive domain of spiritual empowerment. This process will require risk taking to show movement from the negative self to the positive self, and the recognition of God's power to restore. The construction of the bridge demonstrates the process required to reconstruct our attitudes and adjust to a new foundation.

What is happiness in your relationship? Does your happiness depend on how your feelings are received from others? Are you in the habit of denying yourself the joy your life is entitled to? If this is a problem area in your life, it is important for you to release the fear of freedom. You deserve to be happy in your relationship! It is time for you to release the **RACE** syndrome:

1. **R**ejection
2. **A**lienation
3. **C**omplication
4. **E**xperimentation

The RACE syndrome is an extension of personal fear and anxiety used to hinder positive growth in the attitudes of men and women. **Rejection** relates to fear and how it manifests itself in our relationships. Fear of rejection implies one is not at peace in their relationship with others. True feelings cannot be shown because of this fear. **Alienation** relates to a lack of trust. We develop a false sense of security in our personal domains. **Complication** begins to move in on every aspect of our lives because of the barrier of low self-esteem and the feeling of shame and guilt. **Experimentation** is the area of major concern resulting in accepting sin and running away from God and our Christian walk. This prevents socialization skills from achieving full potential and stagnates the opportunity to become a positive influence. If the trust has been violated, learn how to take the risk of restoration of trust. *(Proverbs 3:5,6)*. This is a difficult process to achieve, yet it is not impossible to receive.

The Loaded Question

The question must be asked: Are you prepared to work? If the answer is "yes," then we are able to move to a higher level. The initial step is complete understanding of feelings and overcoming the emotional barrier. It is apparent that working in this area will require complete focus on setting and achieving short-term goals through risk taking *(II Timothy 1:7)*.

The attitude projected during this restoration is important because of the strong sensitivity regarding every aspect of the relationship. The attitude of faith is used like a prescription from a doctor; a daily dose is ingested for strength. The daily interaction through communication should show a different level of sharing feelings and meeting the needs of the relationship.

In difficult areas of communication, the parties involved may require a trained third party to avoid roadblocks. This process will require action steps for attitude change. The action of asking God to move the old self out of the way allows the restoration of the new Christian man and woman to emerge to their full potential.

Now is the time for another attitude change towards prayer and fasting. Throughout the Bible, Jesus has provided Christians with a plan for salvation. Jesus understands our shortcomings and shows us how important it is to communicate with the Holy Spirit during our difficult days. Thank God for the power of Prayer! Through prayer and fasting we allow the Holy Spirit to enter into our lives and help us through trials and tribulations. Christians cannot receive the blessings of victory over Satan without prayer and fasting *(Matthew 17:21)*. The open line of communication will adjust the attitude of the Christian man and woman and allow relationships to create foundations by breaking barriers and building bridges.

Breaking the Stronghold of Anger

Sometimes we move into an unrecognizable anger zone. We allow that anger to consume us, resulting in behaviors that others may reject because of their inability to understand our personal issues.

Without knowing where the anger originated, it continues to manifest into a negative personality and causes depression, isolation, and anxiety.

A Story is told...

One year ago we met a young couple. Elton and Janisse began each day with prayer and were conscientious to say something good about one another. This was a natural beginning to their day. One day Elton went to lunch with some co-workers. He was attracted to a new sports car that caught his eye in the dealership's showroom. His co-workers encouraged him to go in to get a better look, and when Elton got closer, he was excited by the color and the beautiful design. As he continued to admire the automobile, he also noticed the cost and realized it would take all the money he and his wife had saved just for the down payment.

After work, Elton rushed home to share the excitement with Janisse. She also became very excited with his enthusiasm until he mentioned his intentions to use their savings for a down payment. Janisse reminded him their savings was to buy a home someday. The couple quarreled and was unable to agree upon the future of their savings. They slept in separate beds for the first time in their marriage.

During the night, neither could sleep, and it was clear they would not come together regarding this issue. As morning approached, they both thought about their daily routine, who would offer the prayer, and who could say something good about yesterday. The moment had come for the couple to make a decision.

Proverbs 15:1
A soft answer turns away wrath.

Elton prayed, as a tear rolled down his cheek. Then Janisse said to him, "Honey the good thing about you yesterday was the wonderful joy you demonstrated when you told me about the car. Unfortunately, I was...," Before she could finish the thought, her husband interrupted and said, "Honey, the good thing about you yesterday was how you listened to me talk about a dream, but I realized the reality is building my life with you. Somehow the car does not appeal to me anymore." *(Proverbs 4:7)*

Elton became excited about a dream and he was contemplating a selfish decision. Janisse was offended for two reasons, the lack of communication and Elton's not being sensitive towards the family goals and objectives.

Are you demonstrating the kind of sensitivity that will reflect Jesus Christ within your life?

Anger Management

In the story of Elton and Janisse, two points are significant as we investigate the complexities of managing and dealing with anger and other associated feelings.

1. The couple established a routine which became a fortifier against the attack of self-gratification. The daily prayer and a simple, but important exercise of saying something good about each other, made a difference.

2. During a time of weakness, the anger was a result of human tendencies leading to confrontation.

It is accurate to address our feelings regarding how we deal with anger. But what becomes difficult is implementing the behavior change to improve how we can elevate ourselves to handle anger and the anxiety associated with these feelings. Each of us has developed our own method of coping with uncomfortable situations. In the process of understanding the mechanism we develop, it would be helpful if we became open to a personal inventory about who we are, and how we cope. In many situations we cope by avoidance, isolation, depression, and aggression. These methods for coping can create barriers in the way we interact with each other. We must ask ourselves if our coping skills are misleading us in the areas that really matter.

Peter was in the garden of Gethsemane when Jesus was about to be taken away by the Roman soldiers. As the soldiers approached Jesus, Peter reacted by using a sword to strike a servant and cut his ear off. *(Matthew 26:51)* Peter's way of coping with adversity was by using aggression. In his own mind, he felt it was the only response to demonstrate his anger. Just think about having an opportunity to be in the presence of Jesus and be provided instructions, motivation, and Holy wisdom. Yet the teachings of the Lord were not enough to prevent the aggressive behavior of Peter. It was his way of coping with that situation. Jesus wants us to be in control of our emotions, so we can make positive decisions.

The decisions we make in our relationships require constant evaluation of feelings and the considerations of others. The attitude towards relationships must show there is a legitimate love for the other person. In observing couples and relationships in crisis, it is apparent that one person has shut down and has refused to communicate, while the other is frustrated and provides all the communication. The person who continues to talk out of frustration has also developed a sense of cynicism, which is communicated in their demeanor. The person who refuses to communicate has redirected their level of response as a defense mechanism. Both develop a safe place of refuge within their own minds, and refuse to hear what is being conveyed during the conversation.

The inability to be heard and share feelings can materialize into aggression, reflecting the frustration experienced in relationships in crisis. When that happens, it becomes necessary to refocus on making an Attitude Adjustment to reestablish the love and joy of the relationship. The need for a risk taking experience is required. The need to make a change in behavior becomes paramount to change the attitude.

The Lord is willing to improve how we deal with our attitude. He is available to us, just as he was available to Moses, during the parting of the Red Sea. Our relationships, it states, will require the same work to maintain them as it did to gain them. In *Philippians 4:13:* "I can do all things through Christ which strengthened me." Our Attitude Adjustment is not a process that we will face alone. It is a process we face with Christ. Even during the most difficult times when we feel there is no one else to turn to, we can turn to Christ. An even greater comfort to having Christ with us is the understanding that He hears our prayers. We must have faith that He will give us the power to change.

The process of change becomes essential as we recognize the many aspects of sin. God did not intend for us to have contrite spirits and not improve ourselves as Christians. It is imperative for us to understand what it means to develop in our Christian walk. We must be aware of the smallest detail regarding who we are as individuals, and how we project ourselves to others. Our attitude should reflect our Christian experience and the joy should radiate in our conversation and actions *(Ephesians 4: 29-32)*. The difficulty is how we deal with the sins which prevent us from achieving eternal salvation. The negative thoughts, conversations and the inability to forgive appear to manifest itself as major barriers in our relationship with others. Yet, holding onto sin continues to make us comfortable with sin.

If a person shows disrespect to someone during a disagreement and this is a regular behavior, the change process will be difficult work. The difficulty of change can be taken away with the power of the Lord, and faith. Still a change agent is needed and that is the Holy Spirit. The Holy Spirit will direct our path when we submit and let go, and let God handle this process of transformation.

During this transforming experience, we need to understand that our mind, body, and soul must be one. The mind must be steadfast on obtaining new knowledge to increase our capacity to understand and fortify ourselves with the Word of God. Our bodies must be strong to endure the trials and tribulations of change resulting from transition from sinful lifestyles. This becomes exceedingly important for people who have abused their bodies with alcohol, drugs, and improper diets.

We must commune with God through the Holy Spirit by increasing our fasting, meditation and prayer. This is a very essential paradigm change for the Attitude Adjustment of the Christian Man and Woman. In our walk with God, we must realize that He will provide us with what we need. Even at our weakest moment, God can support us and make our lives easier. All that is required of us, is that we have faith.

Personal Notes

Chapter Eight
Preparing for Transition

Expecting the Promise

What type of attitude do you have with others?

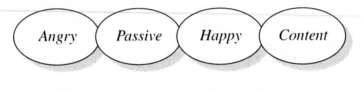

| Angry | Passive | Happy | Content |

_____   _____   _____   _____

Developing a Paradigm For Change...

1. Learn to develop a spiritual connection to God.
2. Learn to be open to each other's uniqueness.
3. Learn how to communicate the right message.
4. Learn how to nurture yourself and others.
5. Learn how to extend yourself to others.
6. Learn to forgive and forget.

**"True Love" is love rooted in God's love. This is why
"True Love Conquers All"**

Philippians 3:13,14
Brethren, I count not myself to have apprehended:
but this one thing I do.
Forgetting these things which are behind,
and reaching forth unto those things which are before.
I press toward the mark for the prize of the high calling of God
in Christ Jesus.

Self Inventory

Are you in Balance with Self and God?
Test Yourself

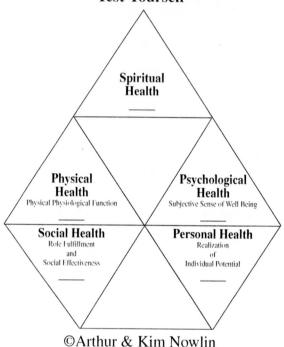

©Arthur & Kim Nowlin

From a numerical perspective, please label each:
Which is most important to you – One is highest; five is lowest

Please label 1-5 of your Self-Inventory

1. _____

2. _____

3. _____

4. _____

5. _____

A story is told...

At the age of eight, Darek became crippled. He would always sit on his front porch and watch the other children play as they ran and jumped and appeared to have a great deal of fun. One day as he watched the children play, he was overcome by extreme sadness. His grandmother came out of the house and asked, "Are you ready for a new adventure that you and I can take together?" Darek smiled and said, "Yes!". She took him to the family doctor, who had made arrangements for him to be seen by a specialist for his particular disability.

The doctor examined Darek and asked him if he would like to ride in a space tunnel. The boy was excited at the thought. The doctor explained, "While you are riding in this tunnel we will have an opportunity to take pictures of every part of your body, and we will see what we need to do to help you walk." Darek's eyes lit up as he asked, "Would God do that for me?" Amazed at the young boy's response, the doctor asked Darek whether he had faith. The little boy looked at the doctor and asked, "What is faith?" "Faith is believing God will help you during the most difficult time of your life; all you need is the faith of a mustard seed." Darek paused. "How big is a mustard seed?" The doctor replied, "it's very small."

Darek thought a moment, then said, "I have faith that God will let me walk like other children, doctor." The doctor smiled and said, "So do I, son." Time passed, and Darek underwent the corrective operation. Shortly thereafter, he began physical therapy. One day, the doctor asked Darek whether he still had faith. Darek replied, "I know God has already healed me because my grandmother has faith too."

Philippians 1:6
... that he which hath begun a good work in you
will perform it until the day of Jesus Christ.

Darek's faith was so strong that everyone in the hospital came to see him take his first steps. As Darek stood to his feet, his grandmother told him to recite *Hebrews 11:1*. **"Now Faith is the substance of things Hoped for and the evidence of things not seen."** He continued to say that scripture over and over. Then the time came for Darek to take his first step. The nurses and doctors cried with gratitude and joy. Darek looked at his grandmother and said, "See grandmother, we had faith."

We must have faith that God can give us an Attitude Adjustment to improve our lives.

Darek's faith grew because he understood what faith was. He didn't question the results because he just believed.

Don't doubt, just believe...

Personal Notes

Chapter Nine
The Access Key

Receiving your fruits

Whenever it appears difficult for you to move to the next level, think about all the wonderful blessings God has waiting for you. When our attitude is not positive, negative reactions and consequences interfere with the blessing process.

God wants and expects our relationships to be enhanced by utilizing the Word of God, prayer, and having a positive interaction with others. He wants and expects us to have an attitude that reflects how He loves us also. The fruits of the Spirit should manifest itself through us, so that our attitude at all times will be pleasing to Him.

Rewards are given to those who demonstrate the "special fruits".
What are these fruits? Galatians 5:22,23

1. _____

2. _____

3. _____

4. _____

5. _____

6. _____

7. _____

8. _____

9. _____

It's Time to Break the Generational Curse

1. *What type of attitude do I project?*

2. *What am I verbalizing?*

3. *What's not being verbalized?*

4. *How did I learn to cope with adversity? Is abuse a symptom associated with my family origin (sexual, verbal, physical, and substance)?*

5. *What is my tone? Is it similar to my mother's or father's?*

6. *Do I have difficulty remaining consistent and in balance with my actions towards others ?*

Helpful scriptures for breaking the curse

Proverbs 14:1
Every wise woman buildeth her house,
but the foolish plucketh it down with her hands.

Proverbs 3:1
My son forget not my laws
but let thine heart keep my commandments.

Proverbs 1:8
My son hear the instruction of thy father,
and forsake not the law of thy mother.

Proverbs 1:7
The fear of the Lord is the beginning of knowledge,
but fools despise wisdom and instruction.

Keys to Receiving the Promise

1. Recognize the Problem
2. Know the Origin of Problem
3. Communicate with God
4. Develop an Action Plan
5. Take a Daily Inventory
6. Visualize Change
7. Take Action
8. Have Faith
9. Expect the Promise

Take Action Over Your Circumstances

1. Learn to listen
2. Develop better communication skills
3. Let go of negative associations
4. Show willingness to change
5. Increase your relationship with God

Your choices will determine where your bridge will take you.

Personal Notes

I Thessalonians 5:17
In your attitude change, pray without ceasing.

Personal Notes

1 Peter 5:6
Humble yourselves therefore under the mighty hand of God that he may exalt you in due time.

Personal Notes

Ephesians 3:20
*Now unto him that is able to do exceeding abundantly above
all that we ask or think, according to the power
that worketh in us.*

_____

_____

_____

_____

_____

_____

_____

_____

_____

_____

_____

_____

About the Authors

Arthur E. Nowlin, MSW, CSW, CAC

Currently serving as Deputy Director of Kim Logan Communications Christian Family Counseling Clinic, Arthur Nowlin has over 15 years of experience in substance abuse counseling and education. He has dedicated his career to working with children and families who have been scarred by the abuse of drugs and alcohol.

He holds a Bachelors of Science Degree in Education and a Masters of Social Work from Wayne State University. He is a certified addictions counselor Level-1 and has received numerous awards and recognition for his work.

Along with his wife, psychologist and professional orator, Kim Logan-Nowlin, they co-founded the "Building Bridges and Breaking Barriers" seminar series focusing on youth development, family crisis, building marriages, and substance abuse counseling. These sessions are team-taught by the Nowlins.

Kim Logan-Nowlin, Ph.D, LPC

Affectionately known to many as "Dr. Kim", Kim Logan-Nowlin is a dynamic speaker who always leaves her audiences spell-bound. She is a gifted woman on a mission to help others discover their gifts. Her message brings encouragement, direction, hope and healing to thousands each year as she travels around the country and abroad giving inspiration to people of all ages.

Dr. Kim is president of Kim Logan Communications, Inc., where she has trained people from all walks of life to "Speak for Success" for the past 20 years.

Her educational background includes holding Bachelors of Science Degrees from Oakwood College and Wayne State University in Special Education; a Masters Degree in Guidance and Family Counseling; and a Doctorate in Speech Communication and Family Counseling from Wayne State University. Dr. Kim has also served as a professor of Speech Communication at WSU, where she graduated with honors and college professor for Wayne County Community College.

Dr. Kim is a licensed professional Christian counselor and communication expert. For many years, she's hosted a "Speak for Success" program on radio and cable television. She has also received numerous awards and recognition for her work with young people.

The Nowlins reside in Detroit, Michigan.

A Word from Arthur Nowlin

We are grateful to have an opportunity to provide you with insight into our "Attitude Adjustment of the Christian Man and Woman." Be encouraged to revisit this book at least once every month to help you stay on track with your transformation, and we ask you:

Are you ready for an Attitude Adjustment of the Christian Man and Woman?

Let us hear of the great work God is doing in your life!!
We are available for you...

How to Reach Us...

Kim Logan Communications, Inc.
8313 Grandriver Avenue
Detroit, Michigan 48204

www.kimlogancommunications.com

E-mail: kaattitudeadjustment@yahoo.com

To order additional copies of
"The Attitude Adjustment of the Christian Man and Woman"
please call us at at (313) 898-8200
or write to the addresses above.

Single orders or larger group orders for churches, businesses,
libraries or schools are welcome!

Printed in the United States
62064LVS00002B/1-150